SQUASH RACQUETS

BROWN

PHYSICAL EDUCATION ACTIVITIES SERIES

Consulting Editor:
AILEENE LOCKHART
University of Southern California
Los Angeles, California

Evaluation Materials Editor:
JANE A. MOTT
Smith College
Northampton, Massachusetts

ARCHERY, Wayne C. McKinney
BADMINTON, Margaret Varner
BADMINTON, ADVANCED, Wynn Rogers
BIOPHYSICAL VALUES OF MUSCULAR ACTIVITY, E. C. Davis,
    Gene A. Logan, and Wayne C. McKinney
BOWLING, Joan Martin
CANOEING AND SAILING, Linda Vaughn and Richard Stratton
CIRCUIT TRAINING, Robert P. Sorani
CONDITIONING AND BASIC MOVEMENT CONCEPTS, Jane A. Mott
CONTEMPORARY SQUARE DANCE, Patricia A. Phillips
FENCING, Muriel Bower and Torao Mori
FIELD HOCKEY, Anne Delano
FIGURE SKATING, Marion Proctor
FOLK DANCE, Lois Ellfeldt
GOLF, Virginia L. Nance and E. C. Davis
HANDBALL, Michael Yessis
JUDO, Daeshik Kim
LACROSSE FOR GIRLS AND WOMEN, Anne Delano
BASKETBALL FOR MEN, Glenn Wilkes
GYMNASTICS FOR MEN, A. Bruce Frederick
MODERN DANCE, Esther E. Pease
PHYSICAL AND PHYSIOLOGICAL CONDITIONING FOR MEN, Benjamin Ricci
SKIING, Clayne Jensen and Karl Tucker
SKIN AND SCUBA DIVING, Albert A. Tillman
SOCCER, Richard L. Nelson
SOCIAL DANCE, William F. Pillich
SOFTBALL, Martin E. Kneer and Charles L. McCord
SQUASH RACQUETS, Margaret Varner and Norman Bramall
SWIMMING, Betty J. Vickers and William J. Vincent
TABLE TENNIS, Margaret Varner and J. R. Harrison
TAP DANCE, Barbara Nash
TENNIS, Joan Johnson and Paul Xanthos
TENNIS, ADVANCED, Chet Murphy
TRACK AND FIELD, Kenneth E. Foreman and Virginia L. Husted
TRAMPOLINING, Jeff T. Hennessy
VOLLEYBALL, Glen H. Egstrom and Frances Schaafsma
WEIGHT TRAINING, Philip J. Rasch
BASKETBALL FOR WOMEN, Frances Schaafsma
GYMNASTICS FOR WOMEN, A. Bruce Frederick
WRESTLING, Arnold Umbach and Warren R. Johnson

1/70

PHYSICAL EDUCATION
ACTIVITIES SERIES

SQUASH
RACQUETS

MARGARET VARNER

The University of Texas at El Paso

NORMAN B. BRAMALL

Haverford College

WM. C. BROWN COMPANY PUBLISHERS

DUBUQUE, IOWA

Printed in the United States of America

Foreword

It gives me great pleasure to write the Foreword for this expertly authored book entitled *Squash Racquets*. The co-authors, Margaret Varner and Norman B. Bramall, are well known in this sport as teachers and competitors. Norman Bramall has developed no less than five national women's singles champions, one of whom is Miss Varner. She has won the national title four times and has represented the United States in international squash racquets, tennis, and badminton competitions. In addition, the co-authors have been outstanding teachers and competitors in the closely related sport of tennis.

This excellent book is appropriately illustrated with sequence photographs of the authors' impeccable stroke patterns and contains numerous line drawings to enhance the reader's understanding of the intriguing angles of squash racquets. The descriptions of how to play the game are clear and concise and make stimulating reading.

Undoubtedly this outstanding book will be a worthy contribution to the literature in physical education as well as to individuals and associations concerned with the game of squash racquets.

MARGARET OSBORNE DUPONT
Former U.S.A., French and Wimbledon
singles and doubles champion in tennis
Former national senior doubles champion
in squash racquets

Preface

The purpose of this book is to provide both the beginning and advanced squash racquets player with an organized description of how best to perform and enjoy the game. The student of squash racquets must learn not only how to execute fundamental techniques but also when and why they should be employed. These questions are discussed herein. Instructions and analyses are accompanied by sequence photographs and illustrative diagrams. Practice drills are outlined. A glossary of terms peculiar to squash racquets, a section on equipment, a description of squash racquets associations and tournaments, and selected references constitute a handy reference for the enthusiast.

Self-evaluation questions are distributed throughout the text. These afford the reader typical examples of the kinds of understanding and levels of skill that should be acquiring as he progresses toward mastery of squash racquets. The player should not only answer the printed questions but should pose additional ones as a self-check on learning. Since the order in which the content of the text is read and the teaching progression of the instructor are matters of individual decision, the evaluative materials are not necessarily positioned according to the presentation of given topics. In some instances the student may find that he cannot respond fully and accurately to a question until he has read more extensively or has gained more playing experience. From time to time he should return to such troublesome questions until he is sure of the answers or has developed the skills called for, as the case may be.

PREFACE

Although this book is designed primarily for college physical education classes, the information is clearly suitable for and useful to the club or tournament player.

Contents

1

What Squash Racquets Is Like

Squash racquets is a game played with racquets and a ball in a rectangular four-wall court. The game gets its name from the sound of the ball (squash) and from the forerunner of squash racquets (Racquets). It is somewhat similar to other four-wall games such as handball and paddle ball. Squash was played on courts of many sizes and descriptions in its early days and it was not until 1911 in England that court dimensions were standardized. Squash racquets achieved great popularity in the United States in the 1920's and 30's although on a smaller court. The game is popular in India, the Far East, Pakistan, Egypt, and South Africa, as well as in Australia and New Zealand where it is played on the larger English size court.

"Squash" is usually played indoors with artificial lighting. There may be one player (singles) or two players on a side (doubles). The game features many angle shots because of the walls and the angle the ball can take off them. The measurements of the singles and doubles courts are shown in Figures 1 and 2. The telltale, a metal strip 17 inches in height from the

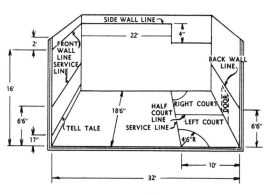

Figure 1—Singles Court.

1

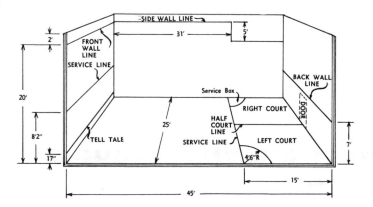

Figure 2—Doubles Court.

floor and 18 feet 6 inches wide on the front wall, functions as a net, i.e., the ball is out of play when it is struck. The red lines around the upper limits of the court are the boundaries. The racquet, which is 27 inches in length with a circular head not over 9 inches in diameter, weighs about 9½ ounces. The ball is a small black, hard rubber ball with a hollow center. Figure 3 shows a fine quality racquet and ball.

A squash game consists of 15 points. The best of five games constitutes a match. The right to serve or receive in the first game of a match is decided by a toss. The winner of a game usually serves first in the next game.

When the score is 13 all in singles and doubles, the side which reaches 13 first has the option of setting the game to three or five, and the side which reaches three or five first then wins the game. If the side elects not to set the score, then 15 remains the game score. If the score has not

Figure 3—Racquets and Ball.

2

been 13 all, the same procedure is followed at 14 all, except that the optional set must be three.

The game is started with an underhand or overarm serve from either service box to the player in the opposite service court. The ball must go directly to the front wall. After the service is completed the ball is "in play" back and forth to the front wall until it hits the telltale, goes out of bounds, or a fault occurs. It may hit any wall on the way to the front wall. Only one bounce on the floor is allowed between strokes. The incoming server has the choice of serving from either box, but if he scores a point he must move to the other box. If the server loses a point, the receiver then becomes the server. In doubles, only one player gets to serve on the side that begins the game before the other team serves. Thereafter both players on a side get to serve. As long as points are scored, the server continues serving. In doubles, only the serving side changes courts when a point is scored. The receivers remain in their same courts to allow the server to serve to the other opponent. Rules must be followed while playing the game, and the "lets" and "faults" which occur during play will be discussed in a later chapter.

Squash racquets has developed in popularity since its early beginnings though it has always been very popular in the British Isles. Countries which were at one time a part of the British Commonwealth were exposed to the game and developed skill in squash racquets. Some of the world's best players have come from Pakistan and Egypt. Australia is taking up the game with a vengeance! Interest is developing in the United States and Canada as more and more leisure time is made possible for the citizens. The service academies consider the game to be a superb conditioner and have courts in their facilities. Squash can be played by both sexes and all ages. The game is stimulating mentally and physically, and it has all the values of individual and team sports. The fact that the walls keep the ball in court most of the time allows rallies to develop early in learning. Nevertheless, concentration and practice are needed to perfect the skills which are necessary to become a really good player.

2

Skills Essential
for Everyone

The center position, the court temperature, the grip, and the use of spin must be understood before the strokes are analyzed. Then, in the early stages of learning, *concentrate on the stroke pattern.* This is initially more important than actually hitting the ball; indeed, the desire to hit the ball can be the great destroyer of the stroke pattern.

THE POSITION AT THE "T" (Figure 4)

The basic position is at the "T," a place just in front of the service line and equidistant from the side walls. It is the easiest location from which to reach the four corners of the court since it is more simple to

run forward than backward (back pedal). If you play your shots correctly, it will be easy to assume this position at the T. On the other hand, badly played shots will force you out of the center of the court and allow your opponent to command the center. You must earn the privilege of taking this ideal center position with well executed strokes and carefully controlled shots. The position will vary slightly according to your opponent's position.

COURT TEMPERATURE

The temperature of the court affects the temperature of the ball, and, as will be explained in a later chapter, the temperature of the ball affects the type of game to be played. Courts which are heated or air-

Figure 4—Position at the "T".

Evaluation Questions

Can you take the correct grip and then bounce the ball on each side of the racquet without missing for 10, 15, and then 20 times? With the same grip, can you alternate sides of the racquet for each stroke?

conditioned maintain a relatively consistent temperature. Unheated courts are subject to natural temperature changes. A hot court causes the ball to have more action, that is, to rebound vigorously off the walls. A cold court will deaden the ball, giving less rebound off the walls. For example, a shot played two feet above the telltale on a cold court will bounce about midcourt; a shot played identically on a hot court will carry to backcourt and rebound off the back wall. Manufacturers are now developing a ball whose bounce will not be affected by the warm-up and constant use. Balls have already been developed for cold courts and hot courts. Nevertheless, a ball selected for use on a hot court still has more action at a higher temperature.

The temperature of the ball increases as it is used. The harder and more often it is struck, the more it heats up. This fact has strategic implications.

THE GRIP (Figure 5)

The most important first technique to master is the correct grip. One grip, with slight variations, can be used for all the strokes.

The grip in squash racquets resembles the Continental grip in tennis in that the point of the "V" formed by the thumb and forefinger is slightly to the left of the top of the handle. The handle lies diagonally across the fingers and palm allowing the third finger and little finger to maintain a firm hold. The fingers, particularly the forefinger, are comfortably spread. More wrist action is achieved if the racket is held near the end; a firm wrist is possible if the handle is held further from the end. The wrist is kept firm on practically all strokes with the exception of the

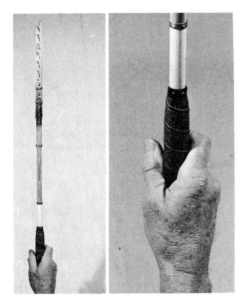

Figure 5—The Grip.

forehand drive. Both variations of the basic grip will be valuable in producing the various strokes. Hold the racquet quite firm at impact when executing power shots and hold it more loosely on the touch shots. The Continental grip allows the wrist to cock back in the proper direction, putting the face of the racquet at the correct angle throughout the stroke.

SPIN

This grip adjusts the angle of the face of the racquet so that imparting underspin to the ball is facilitated. To impart underspin, the face of the racquet must swing from high to low as it chops or cuts under the ball. This action will cause the ball to rotate backward toward the player as it goes to the target. A ball with underspin will angle more sharply and pull down to the floor after hitting the front wall more quickly than one without spin.

Shots with spin are easier to control than spinless shots, but spin diminishes speed. Some shots require more speed while some require more spin.

Strokes made on the right side of a right-handed player are forehand strokes. Those made on the left side are backhand strokes. The side wall to his right is referred to as the forehand wall and the wall to his left as the backhand wall. (All statements in this book refer to right-handed players; left-handed players should reverse the instructions.) All strokes can be either forehand or backhand, although serves are seldom hit with a backhand stroke.

THE LOB SERVE (Figures 6, 7, and 8)

The lob serve is the stroke that begins each play. Legally it can be played underhand or overhand, but the usual method is underhand on the forehand side.

To lob serve from the right service box, take the aforementioned grip with the racquet hand and hold the ball in the other hand. Stand with

Figure 6—The Lob Serve from the Right Box.

Figure 7—The Lob Serve from the Left Box.

the right foot in the service box and with the left step toward the middle of the court and as far forward as possible in what is called an open stance. The right foot must remain in contact with the floor until the ball is contacted. By standing near the center of the court and contacting the ball as far away as possible from the side wall, the angle to the front wall is lessened and it becomes easier to direct the ball to the intended area. Take care to place your feet properly and hold this position momentarily. Now look toward the front wall at the target spot you wish to hit, then look back at the ball. The hand and racquet start together well in front of the body. The ball is tossed up about one to three inches high, well in front of the body, as the backswing is taken down and back. The wrist is firm and not flicked as the arm swings forward to meet the ball directly ahead of the body at about knee level. The contact point is under the ball so that it will loft upwards. The racquet, arm, and shoulder all follow the ball, allowing a long, high, deliberate follow-through. To obtain the correct angle to the side wall the ball should strike the front wall slightly to the left of center. The ball will leave the front wall at about the same angle as it approaches. It should contact the front wall as high as possible and have a rising, arching effect after leaving it. The more the ball rises after hitting the front wall and the higher it travels, the more likely it is to fall perpendicularly in the back corner. Serves dropping in this downward fashion are extremely difficult to return. No spin is intentionally imparted to the lob serve.

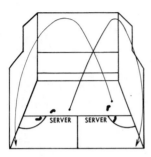

Figure 8—Flight Patterns of the Lob Serve.

To lob serve from the left service box, step to the center of the court as far as possible. Stand comfortably with the body in a stationary position, left side to the front wall. This foot position is called an exaggerated closed stance. All elements of stroking from the left are the same as from the right. The point of aim on the front wall will vary, since it is possible to stand nearer the center of the court from the left side. By contacting the ball closer to center, the point of aim will be several feet to the right of center.

A good lob serve from either side should have the following characteristics. After striking the front wall it should loft or rise upward as it loops to the side wall, where it slithers along the wall and drops downward with very little speed into the back corner. If played at a bad angle, it will bump off the side wall toward the center of the court. If played with too much speed it will rebound off the back wall. There should be as little "action" off the side and back walls as possible. The receiver will have difficulty returning the serve because the wall will interfere with his stroking. Remember that the rebound of the ball varies with the temperature of the ball.

Perfection of a good lob serve is imperative as it forces your opponent to be on the defensive and earns you the center of the court ready to attack. Generally speaking, it is more effective when served to your opponent's backhand.

THE FOREHAND AND BACKHAND DRIVES (Figures 9 and 10)

A drive is a powerful stroke played after the ball has bounced, and it is used to "drive" the opponent to a back corner. It can be played as a wall shot or a crosscourt shot. If its length is perfect, it is an outright winner.

The forehand drive begins with the racquet in front of and close to the body with the head of the racquet up and the left hand on the shaft. The backswing is taken with the upper part of the arm close to the body. The racquet head is moving back at shoulder or face level to a position about waist level behind the body. The wrist is being cocked and the shoulders are turning as the head of the racquet leads back. The upper part of the arm remains close to the body, and the lower arm and racquet swing forward with great force to contact the ball at the height of the tin. Level off the height of the ball at the top of the tin. Play the ball close to your body to mask it from your opponent and yet not restrict a free swing. More wrist power is used on this stroke than on any other. The shoulders rotate forward with the forward swing of the arm. The racquet is swung in the direction in which the ball is intended, although the force of the stroke will carry the follow-through sufficiently. The follow-through should never come above shoulder height. The body remains in the semicrouched position on the follow-through to give control to the stroke. The entire stroke should be continuous, compact, controlled, and explosive. Big, wild swings do not permit control and are a danger to the opponent.

The feet usually face forward before the drive begins. The right foot is pivoted and takes the weight as the body is turning to the side. The left foot steps diagonally forward, and the weight is transferred to it with the forward swing of the racquet. The knees are bent and the hips flexed throughout the stroke.

9

Figure 9—Forehand Drive.

Figure 10—Backhand Drive.

Most important to all stroking is keeping the eyes directly on the ball in order to achieve a solid contact in the center of the racquet. This improves the timing which is so essential for power and crisply stroked shots. Peripheral vision will give you an idea of your opponent's position in the court, so keep your eye on the ball!

The backhand drive is played just as the forehand except that the wrist is firm and the shoulders turned slightly more to allow a free swing of the arm, otherwise the backswing is inhibited. Because the stroking arm on the backhand is on the side of the body closest to the front wall, the ball must be contacted sooner.

A wall shot is a shot started from one side of the court which remains on that side of the court. (See Figures 11 and 12.) "A" refers to

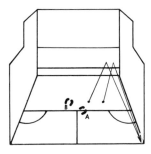

Figure 11—Fore-
hand Wall Shot.

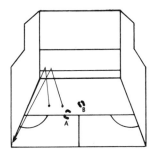

Figure 12—Back-
hand Wall Shot.

the stroker; "B" to the stroker's opponent. A crosscourt shot, Figure 13, starts on one side and crosses over to the other side of the court. For example, a wall shot played with a forehand drive skims back along the wall to the forehand rear corner. A crosscourt shot played with the forehand angles to and from the front wall and ends up in the backhand corner. The choice of whether a forehand drive should be played as a wall shot or as a crosscourt shot will depend upon the location of your opponent in relation to you. The body must be well turned to the side to play a wall shot. The feet should be parallel to each other and point to the side wall in a closed stance. To crosscourt, the stance is changed by pulling the left foot back into an open stance. The body faces the front wall slightly. Shots which are crosscourted should be contacted sooner than those played straight along the wall.

A good wall shot is one that stays very close to the side wall and forces the opponent to the back corner, a defensive position. The higher

From points A and B, where should the ball strike the front wall for a deep wall shot? a deep crosscourt?

Evaluation Questions

DEEP WALL SHOT AND CROSSCOURT SHOT

the ball is hit on the front wall, the deeper it will go in the court. A drive with good length is one that dies in the back corner and does not rebound off the back wall. Wall shots to avoid (Figure 14) are those rebounding off the side wall into the center of the court because of a poor angle of the ball to the front wall and those played too high off the front wall, causing the ball to rebound off the side and back walls and into the center. Shots that break out into the center allow your opponent to take the center of the court, and you are forced into a position behind the opponent—a highly undesirable circumstance!

The exact spot at which the ball contacts the front wall, that is, the height from the floor and distance from the side wall, is therefore of utmost importance. A good general rule to follow in determining your point of aim is to ascertain the distance from the contact point of the ball and racquet to the side wall. Half this figure is the distance the point of aim should be on the front wall. For example, if you contact the ball six feet out from the side wall, it should hit the front wall three feet from the same side wall in order to keep the ball from "breaking" the side wall. Figures 11 and 12 give examples of variations of the point of contact on the front wall. Figure 14 shows an incorrect choice of front wall contact, with the ball breaking towards center.

The forehand and backhand drives may be crosscourted as well as played parallel to the wall. A good crosscourt will have speed, correct angle, and good length. The point of aim on the front wall will be determined by how far forward or back your opponent is in the court.

Diagram A:

DEEP WALL SHOT AND
CROSSCOURT SHOT

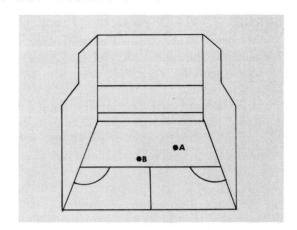

(See Figure 13.) A poorly played crosscourt with no speed and incorrect angle will be returned by the opponent before the ball ever gets behind him or reaches the back corner. The ball should hit the side wall at a point behind your opponent. It generally is a good idea to wait until the opponent is pulled out of center and to one side of the court before attempting the crosscourt to the opposite side. A common fault of inexperienced and unthinking players is continually crosscourting and breaking the ball off the side wall too soon, causing it to go to the middle of the court. (See Figure 15.) Remember that the ball will leave the front wall at about the same angle as it approached.

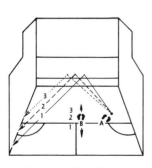

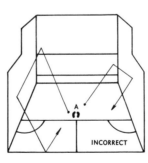

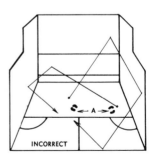

Figure 13—Cross-
court Shots.

Figure 14—Wall
Shots to Avoid.

Figure 15—Cross-
court Shots to
Avoid.

13

CORNER SHOTS (Figures 16, 17, and 18)

A corner shot is a controlled shot played to the near side wall, rebounding to the front wall, and then bouncing on the floor. It strikes the side wall near the front wall, crosses a corner, strikes the front wall just above the telltale, and angles directly to the floor. It should carry an excessive amount of underspin to make it hit the floor as soon as possible. Most corners are played from an area around the service line or forward since it is essential that your opponent be behind you when it is played. A well played corner shot should win the point.

The stroke is similar to the drive, particularly in footwork and body position. Shorten the backswing. Do not float the shot. The wrist flexes on the backswing, comes forward at contact, and is straight on the follow-through. The wrist is responsible for the proper angle for the corner. Wrist action also provides needed deception. The ball may be contacted slightly later since it is going to the wall nearest you. Impart spin by chopping under the ball with an open-faced racquet. Direct the ball to the side wall and follow through with the racquet pointing to

Figure 16—Backhand Corner Shot.

the side wall. If the ball goes to the side wall at about a 45-degree angle, it will terminate at the desired spot.

Take special care to note where your opponent (B) is standing when a corner is attempted. For example, on the forehand side your opponent should be to the right and behind you. On the backhand side, your opponent will be on your left. Remember to play the ball into the wall closest to your opponent since it will rebound to the opposite side of the court.

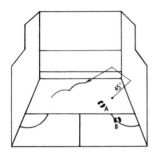

Figure 17—Fore-
hand Corner Shot.

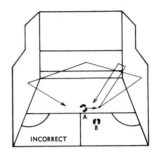

Figure 18—Corner
Shots to Avoid.

A crisply played corner shot that is well angled and with correct speed and spin should hit the front wall just above the telltale and bounce twice before hitting the opposite side wall, provided your opponent fails to reach it after one bounce, in which case it is "not-up" or "down."

A corner played incorrectly will terminate in the center of the court which will force you back behind your opponent. If the ball goes too high and has too much speed, and goes to the side wall at considerably more or less than a 45-degree angle, undesirable complications result.

THE VOLLEY (Figures 19 and 20)

The volley is a stroke played before the ball has bounced on the floor. At midcourt, it usually is played coming directly from the front wall. From a deeper position in the court, it often is played as it comes off the side wall, particularly as a return of service.

The volley stroke is shorter than the drive. Because the ball has not been allowed to bounce, there is less time to turn the body and swing. A shorter stroke therefore results. Quickness of eye and hand are

Figure 19—Forehand Volley.

Figure 20—Backhand Volley.

essential. Ideally, the shoulders are rotated back, particularly on the backhand side, and the step is diagonally forward as the stroke is made. The racquet starts in front of the body and is taken back high alongside the head. The backswing seldom comes farther back than the shoulders. From a position at head and shoulder height the racquet comes forward, down and under the ball. With the face of the racquet open, underspin is imparted to the ball. The swing is made entirely to the side and front of the body.

The volley can be played down the wall or crosscourt, short or long, cornered or crosscornered, depending on your opponent's court position. Remember, however, that a crosscourt shot must be hit sooner than a wall shot. The volley is a very valuable technique because the ball is intercepted before it goes to the back wall, which leaves you at the desired location in the center of the court rather than in the back corner. You will have less time to make a volley, but you will shorten the time your opponent has to reach your return. See Figures 37, 38, and 39 in Chapter 4.

CONDITIONING AND FOOTWORK

To be able to produce the strokes and withstand the fast and long rallies that are the outcome of well played squash a player must be sufficiently conditioned.

To improve endurance, a running pattern similar to footwork used in game play is desirable. (See Figure 21.) Start at the T with racquet in hand and run to each corner and to both sides of the court. Touch your racquet to the wall at floor level and return to center. The footwork and body position should simulate that used in a game. For example, when running forward to the right front corner, crouch and assume a position similar to a forehand shot. Then move back (to the T) while still facing the front wall. Under no circumstances should a player turn around and face the back wall when returning to center. A misdirected shot can be dangerous! When moving to either side wall, first pivot on the foot toward the direction you wish to move. For example, on the backhand side, pivot with the left foot, step right, step left, and step right. Back pedal to center. To move to the backhand corner, pivot left, skip step right-left, and step right. Back pedal to center in about the same fashion. Run quickly through the entire circuit. At first attempt, run the circuit three or four times without stopping. Each day increase the number. The value of correct footwork done quickly in good balance and with

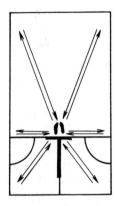

Figure 21—Footwork and Conditioning Drill.

control cannot be underestimated. Haphazard, noisy, and uncontrolled running is characteristic of novice players.

The warm-up before a match helps to get your eye on the ball and to determine the temperature and action of the ball on the particular court. It also helps increase the body temperature in preparation for maximum performance; therefore, get your feet moving and change your position forward and back. Don't be guilty of a lethargic, casual approach to the game!

The winner of a match between two players of equal ability often depends on fitness and endurance. Superb endurance is the reward of repeated, exhausting effort. Rope jumping increases endurance as well as develops lightness of footwork. Although special exercises are valuable to strengthen weak muscles, performance of the game is the best over-all training for the sport.

3

Better Players
Master These Techniques

Additional strokes are fun to experiment with in combination with the essential skills described in Chapter 2. Descriptions of overarm serves, the drop shot, the crosscorner shot, the lob, the boast, and the bow will be found in this chapter. Many of these strokes are slightly more difficult to execute than the basic ones, so these should be learned after the basic strokes. To be able to employ these strokes constitutes a threat; they could be used any time. The fact that your opponent must be alert to this possibility further makes the use of basic strokes more effective.

OVERARM SERVES (Figures 22 and 23)

The overarm serve is played from a position above the shoulder. It is never played with a backhand. It is a secondary serve used to change the style of play, to exploit an opponent's weakness, or to surprise an opponent. It takes considerable experience to determine the best time to employ this variation of serve.

To serve overarm from the right service box, start with the racquet in front of the body and step forward toward the side wall with the right foot in the inside corner of the box. At the same time, turn the shoulders and body to the side and take a high backswing above and behind the head. Drop the racquet behind the back in preparation for the forward swing. Step forward toward the front wall with the left foot. Then swing the racquet forward and contact the ball at a point slightly above head height and to the right but as far forward in the court as possible. The closer you are to the point on the front wall at which you

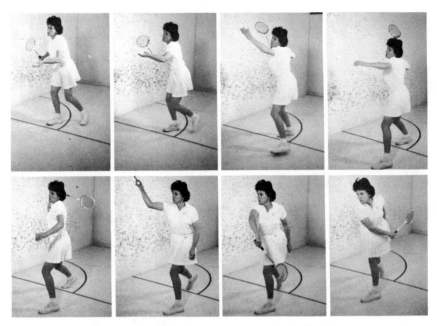

Figure 22—Overarm Serve from Right Box.

Figure 23—Overarm Serve from Left Box.

are aiming, the better your accuracy. The follow-through will come down and across the body.

The overarm serve may be played as a slice serve, that is, one with sidespin and underspin or as a powerful flat serve with speed. (See Figures 24 and 25.)

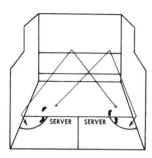

Figure 24—Overarm
Slice Serve.

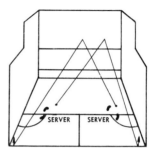

Figure 25—Overarm
Hard Serve.

The *overarm slice serve* has some sidespin and some underspin. To produce these, the racquet face must move from high to low along the right side of and then under the ball. Control is most essential, speed less essential. The front wall usually is contacted just above the service line and slightly to the left of center. The ball rebounds to the side wall, contacting it not more than one foot above the floor at about the service line. It angles sharply to the floor. A good amount of spin on the ball helps bring the ball sharply down into the court close to the side wall. Because the ball lands just beyond the service line and off the side wall, it is very difficult to volley. A ball with spin on it is more difficult to hit than one without spin. A nick is a ball which hits the crease, the place where the side wall and the floor meet. It is unreturnable and occurs occasionally on this type of serve.

The overarm slice serve from the left service box is similar to the slice serve from the right service box, except that from the left side of the court, it is possible to contact the ball at a point farther away from the left side wall, that is, closer to the center. The point of aim on the front wall, therefore, will differ. It will be closer to the side wall than the slice from the right court. How high the ball should hit on the front wall depends on the temperature. Repeated practice and experimentation will aid in determining the correct spot to hit in order to obtain the

Can you overarm serve and keep the ball on the side wall or in the corner 50 per cent of the time? 60 per cent? 70 per cent?

Evaluation Questions

desired results. A serve that is hit too high on the side wall with speed will go on to the back wall and out into the center of the court. The receiver then backs the server against the side wall in order to get in position and have room to stroke. It is better to contact the side wall too low than too high. The disadvantage in this serve is that it is difficult to execute and the receiver is near the center of the court instead of in a back corner. The effectiveness of your serve can be measured by the ease or difficulty your opponent experiences in returning it!

The *overarm hard serve* is stroked in the same manner as other overarm serves except that it should be hit flat without any spin in order to get the necessary speed. For deception, the backswing should be identical with the slice serve. At contact, the face of the racquet will be parallel with the front wall, and the contact point will be behind the ball rather than to the side or under the ball.

The hard serve contacts the front wall from two to three feet above the service line, but this spot again depends upon the temperature. The hard serve travels directly to the back wall, hits the back wall just above the floor, and comes out close to and parallel to the side wall for a short distance. Unless the hard serve has extreme speed, it can be volleyed. Court temperature must always be considered as must the hitting power of the server. A hard serve played on a very cold court will not have enough speed to be effective. On the other hand, on a warm court, it can be devastating.

A variation of the hard serve is the *surprise serve* (Figure 26). Stroke production is identical. The difference lies in the contact point on the front wall and change of direction. The ball is slammed across the court to the front wall near the side wall. It immediately hits the side wall, cuts across in front of the receiver and bounces in the inside front corner of the service court. This serve not only has speed but approaches the receiver at an awkward angle. It is used to fluster and rush him into a poor return. It is useful against a player who reacts slowly or is nervous.

Experiment with the various auxiliary serves to see which ones are best for you. Your success will depend partly upon the ability of the receiver to return the serve. Determine whether his forehand or backhand is better and which serves are more difficult for him to return. Use different serves on different players, depending upon their capabilities.

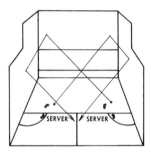

Figure 26—Surprise Serve.

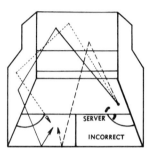

Figure 27—Serves to Avoid.

Guard against incorrectly angled serves (Figure 27). Serves which have no speed, no spin, and terminate in the middle of the court should be avoided. Make the walls your friend by keeping the ball close to them, thereby inhibiting your opponent's stroking. The national champion cannot hurt you if the ball is flush on the wall!

THE DROP SHOT (Figures 28, 29, and 30)

The drop shot is a stroke which causes the ball to drop short in the front of the court. It can be played straight or crosscourt.

The similarity of grip and feet and body positions to other strokes gives the deception necessary to make the drop shot effective. Since it is not a power, but a touch stroke, the backswing and follow-through are abbreviated to eliminate speed. Contact the ball in front of the body about 17 inches above the floor and send it on a direct line to the front wall. There is a great deal of underspin. The body is well crouched, particularly on the follow-through. This gives the necessary control.

23

Figure 28—Forehand Drop Shot.

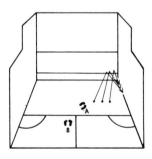

Figure 29—Fore-
hand Drop Shot—
Straight.

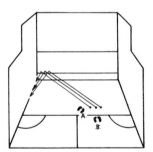

Figure 30—Fore-
hand Drop Shot—
Crosscourt.

Be sure your opponent is behind you when attempting a drop shot. Whether you play it straight or crosscourt depends on the location of your opponent. The angle to the front wall varies with your position in the court. A perfect drop shot would nick in the crease. A badly played drop shot is one played too high above the telltale or one which hits the side wall and bounds away from the wall before hitting the floor. Balls staying close to the wall are exasperating to try to hit!

THE CROSSCORNER (Figure 31)

The crosscorner shot, often called the reverse corner, is a shot played when your opponent is behind and to one side of you. It crosses in front of the body to the side wall and then to the front wall in the far front corner. When a corner or crosscorner is played, the object is to win the point on that shot, since these shots are usually played after the opponent has been maneuvered to a position behind the stroker.

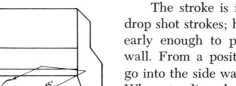

Figure 31—Back-hand Crosscorner.

The stroke is identical with the corner and drop shot strokes; however, the ball must be met early enough to pull it across to the far side wall. From a position at the T the ball should go into the side wall at about a 45-degree angle. When standing closer than this to the front wall, it should go more directly into the side wall. From deep court it will angle into the side wall at less than a 45-degree angle. The angle will vary every time your location in the court changes. Experience will help you learn the correct angle. Success and failure are wonderful teachers!

The crosscorner has its advantages because with the opponent behind, he cannot see the ball as it crosses in front of you and therefore will be late moving to the ball. The shot eventually ends in front of you. The quickness of the shot does not give your opponent time to see the ball, much less get around you to attempt a return. Many lets occur in this type of situation although it is the responsibility of the stroker to step out of the way of his opponent; if your opponent is behind you and your shots are well played, he should be unable to retrieve them despite the fact you step out of his way and give him a clear run to the ball. The exception occurs when the court is very warm and the ball is vigorously bounding off the walls.

THE LOB

The lob is the most valuable defensive stroke with which to "get out of trouble." It is similar to the lob serve for it is a high, slow, deep shot.

It gives you time to regain your balance and position. It is also used as a return of serve to force your opponent to a back corner. Stroked with a forehand or backhand, directed down the wall or crosscourt, and played from front court or backcourt, it is a very valuable weapon. It has exceptionally fine usage in doubles.

The lob stroke is a combination of the lob serve and drive strokes when played from deep court with time to stroke. Played from the forecourt with little time, a flick of the wrist is all that is involved. On both strokes, the racquet must be under the ball at contact to project the ball upwards.

Try to keep the lob close to the walls with the correct speed and angle to insure good length. A lob "out in the open" can be volleyed for a winner.

THE BOAST (Figure 32)

The boast is a little used powerful shot usually made in desperation! It is played from either back corner and hits the side wall first, then the diagonally opposite front corner, striking the front wall and then the floor. A perfectly played boast angles upwards into the side wall at 45 degrees, contacts the front wall just above the telltale, and nicks at the crease. A badly played boast never reaches the front wall or it hits too high or at the wrong angle on the front wall and bounces toward the center of the court.

In addition to the fact the boast is difficult to execute, it takes time for the ball to travel the distance to the front wall, and your opponent at the T has time to retrieve it. Also, as soon as it is obvious that you are struggling an alert opponent anticipates a desperation shot. Unless this shot is hit perfectly it can be a boomerang.

THE BOW (Figure 33)

The bow is the other shot used when there is no alternative. It is very similar to the boast except that it hits the side wall first, the opposite side wall next, then glances almost parallel to the front wall and finally the floor. In order to make the ball hit the opposite side wall before the front wall, it must be angled into the side wall in deep court at about 60 degrees. It also must be hit upwards into the side wall. It is even more difficult to execute than the boast and an element of luck is involved when it does score. Very little time should be spent practicing either the boast or the bow. If the other shots are perfected, the number of times a desperation shot is needed will be diminished.

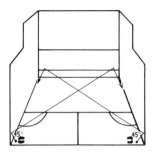

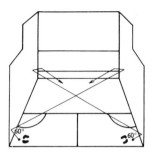

Figure 32—The Boast.   *Figure 33—The Bow.*

WATCHING THE BALL

No techniques, footwork, or strategy can be effectively employed unless the ball is carefully scrutinized all the time. Timing and accuracy depend on this. Watch the ball for safety's sake. Keep an eye on your opponent too, because where he is, the ball is. The idea is to see the start of his play from his racquet rather than first seeing the ball at the front wall.

Face forward when your opponent is behind you and turn only your head. Some players like to keep their racquets high to protect their faces when the opponent is behind; some attempt to protect themselves from the ball or racquet follow-through by elevating a shoulder.

Progress Can
Be Speeded Up

The first step in learning squash racquets, after understanding the how and why of stroke pattern development, is actual stroke practice. Have a plan and practice with intelligence. Seven good self-practice drills and five practice-partner drills are described here.

SELF-PRACTICE DRILLS

Because of the walls a squash player can practice shots as they are played in the game by setting them up to himself. This cannot be done in tennis or badminton.

The - - - line on each self-practice drill represents a set-up. A set-up places the ball in the correct location so that a particular shot can be practiced. The ● indicates the contact point of the ball and racquet. The ——— line is the desired direction and angle of the shot being practiced.

Wall Shot Drill (Figure 34)

SET-UP: Toss the ball about head height onto the side wall near the front wall and let it bounce on the floor.

OBJECT: To stroke a forehand or backhand drive parallel to the side wall with control. No attempt is made to hit the ball continuously.

HINTS: Note closely the angle the ball takes to and from the front wall. Begin with a short swing and gradually move back in the court as your proficiency increases. Practice the same drill on the backhand side.

Forecourt Wall Shot and Crosscourt Shot Drill (Figure 35)

SET-UP: Hit the ball any place on the front wall.

OBJECT: To play a wall shot or crosscourt shot effectively from the attacking area in the forecourt.

HINTS: Note the height of the drive on the front wall which is necessary in order to get correct length. Make certain the ball hits the side wall behind the service box after hitting the floor. For variation, the ball may be aimed just above the telltale to attempt a winner. Gradually move back as accuracy increases.

Backcourt Wall Shot and Crosscourt Shot Drill (Figure 36)

SET-UP: Serve the ball so it rebounds off the back wall.

OBJECT: To play a wall shot or crosscourt drive effectively from a defensive position in deep court.

HINTS: To get depth, move towards the back wall and follow the ball as it goes to and from the back wall. Elevate the ball on the front wall. Vary the drive with a lob.

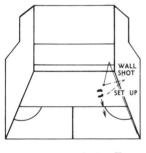

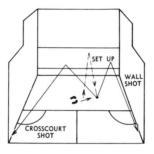

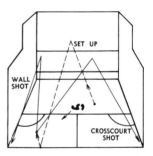

| *Figure 34—Wall Shot Drill.* | *Figure 35—Forecourt Wall Shot and Cross- court Drill.* | *Figure 36—Back- court Wall Shot and Crosscourt Drill.* |

Volley Drill (A) (Figure 37)

SET-UP: Toss the ball to yourself and forehand volley it to the front wall and then volley continuously.

OBJECT: To increase reflex action. Begin by starting away from the front wall at the T and gradually move closer to increase the tempo.

HINTS: Volley with a straight forehand first, then backhand straight. As skill increases, crosscourt the volleys. Vary your position towards the side walls to make the drill more game-like.

Volley Drill (B) (Figure 38)

SET-UP: Lob serve the ball on the front wall to the forehand or backhand side in the forecourt.

OBJECT: To volley the ball just above the telltale for a winner.

HINTS: Do not hit the side wall at any time. Meet the ball as soon as possible. The tempo can be speeded up by using an overarm serve to start the drill. Vary the direction to the front wall to make the drill more game-like.

Volley Drill (C) (Figure 39)

SET-UP: Lob the ball deep to the forehand or backhand with and without hitting the side wall.

OBJECT: To volley the ball deep in order to force the opponent to a back corner.

HINTS: For depth, hit the ball with less underspin.

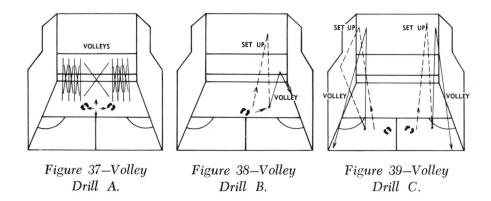

Figure 37—Volley Drill A.

Figure 38—Volley Drill B.

Figure 39—Volley Drill C.

Back Wall Drill (Figure 40)

SET-UP: Serve the ball overarm to the backwall. It may or may not hit the side wall before the back wall.

OBJECT: To learn the action of a ball rebounding off the back wall. As proficiency develops, vary the speed and direction of the set-up.

HINTS: Practice all of the shots on this type of set-up.

PRACTICE-PARTNER DRILLS

Locate a colleague who wants to improve his game and is willing to cooperate in practicing. The practice for both players is most satisfactory if partners are of equal ability, and both can profit from these drills.

The type of shot is labeled on each stroke in the illustration of the drill.

Serve and Return of Serve Drill (Figure 41)

DESCRIPTION: Serve and repeat a particular serve (—) until it is effective from both courts. Then practice another type of serve. A particular type of return (- - -) should also be practiced until it is perfected. Notice that some serves force the receiver to make a certain type of return.

HINTS: If the ball is out away from the wall, go for a winner. If close to the wall, try to make a return that is not a set-up and one that can at least "keep you in the game." Equalize the situation. The two shots played more often than any others in squash are the serve and the return of serve. They should be the most effective, and therefore practiced more diligently than the other shots.

Crosscourt Shot Drill (Figure 42)

DESCRIPTION: A and B are in basic positions to warm-up before a match. These positions should be moved forward and back in order to crosscourt the ball from various places on the court. The object is to crosscourt the ball repeatedly and to hit the opposite side wall anywhere behind the service box for correct length. Your partner will intercept the ball with a drive or volley before it hits the side wall but correctness of angle can be determined. Change positions with your partner in order to practice equally with the forehand and backhand. During an actual game your opponent would be in the center or towards your side of the court which would make the angle you are practicing very effective.

HINTS: Keep the rally going and learn to play the ball at various heights on the front wall with varying amounts of speed to reach your objective. Check the temperature!

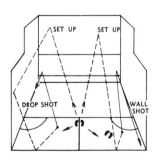
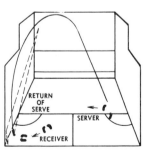
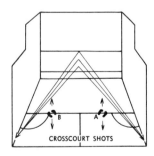

Figure 40—Back Wall Drill.

Figure 41—Serve and Return of Serve Drill.

Figure 42—Crosscourt Shot Drill.

Can you return a set-up parallel to the side wall 4 out of 5 times from the forecourt? 3 out of 5 times from midcourt and back-court?

Evaluation Questions

Crosscourt Drive and Wall Shot Drill (Figure 43)

DESCRIPTION: A and B are practicing the previous crosscourt drill. When either player, A in this illustration, hits a badly angled cross-court, B then has the privilege of playing a wall shot. Wall shots are nearly impossible to practice with a partner but this arrangement does give opportunity.

HINTS: If possible, B returns his own wall shot back to A and keeps the rally going. If B's wall shot is perfect, however, it will be unreturnable. The quality of the shot thus is obvious.

Crosscourt Drive and Crosscorner Drill (Figure 44)

DESCRIPTION: A and B agree that one will crosscourt and the other will crosscorner. After a few minutes they may change shots and also

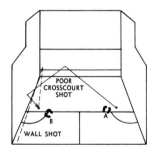

Figure 43—Cross-court Drive and Wall Shot Drill.

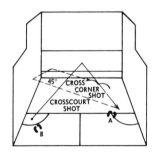

Figure 44—Crosscourt Drive and Crosscorner Drill.

Evaluation Question

> Can you and your partner rally the ball consistently crosscourt without "breaking" the ball off the side wall?

change sides to practice forehand and backhand of both shots. After one player crosscorners, he should attempt to retrieve the ball with a crosscourt shot back to his partner in order to keep the drill continuous.

HINTS: By mutual agreement, elevate the crosscourt drive. The other player then can volley the ball down the wall or crosscorner.

Four Stroke Drill

DESCRIPTION: This drill makes the practice game-like. The effectiveness of the first three or four shots involved in a point should be carefully analyzed. The object is to determine whether you have rightfully gained the position at the T after each shot.

HINTS: The quality of the serve and return of serve set the pattern the play will take. Shots breaking off the side wall and into the center of the court allow your opponent to maintain the center position.

If you are fortunate enough to take private lessons from a professional, he will set up the ball in somewhat the same fashion as you set it up for yourself. He will also provide coach-pupil practice drills. A coach scrimmaging with you can pick out strong and weak points. He might also be willing to observe you under match conditions. If possible, by all means seek some coaching to insure that your game develops in an orthodox fashion.

Apply yourself to the game with enthusiasm and enjoy fellowship with other players. The hours of "want to do" outweigh the hours of "must do."

33

5

Patterns of Play

The techniques described previously are molded into distinct and various patterns in order to develop effective strategy.

SINGLES STRATEGY

Attack and Defense (Figure 45)

The forecourt is the attacking and shot making area. The point-winning shots played most often from in front of the service line are the volley, corner, drop shot, crosscorner, and drive. All of these aggressive shots contact the front wall just above the telltale and so can be unretrievable. Deep drives and lobs can be played from the forecourt as well, but they are used when your location in relationship to your opponent's is unsafe to attempt a short winner.

Occasionally a player with exceptionally good control can effectively play corners and drop shots from deep court. Because they are unexpected from a defensive position, they can be successful. If both players have been forced to the backcourt, a winning shot will have a better chance of being successful. Rarely should a drop shot or corner shot be attempted when your opponent is in the center of the court.

The backcourt is the defensive and transposition area. Transposition means to "exchange in position." You want to change from a defensive to an attacking player in order to score and at the same time force your opponent to defend. Shots which can be used to transpose your position are drives, volleys, and particularly lobs—low and high. Drives and volleys must contact the front wall well above the telltale to carry to deep court.

Figure 45—Shot Making and Transposition Areas.

The lob, which has less speed, must contact the front wall well above the service line. Unless these shots are kept very close to the wall, an eager opponent will volley them and you will remain behind in a defensive area!

The Serve

The serve begins the play so give special attention to it so you can get a good start. Serves are often more effective to the opponent's backhand. (Don't forget to note when you are playing a left-hander!) Vary your serve if this proves effective but if a serve is scoring for you, continue using it. Remember that the lob serve takes less energy and in a long, close match, this may be the determining factor. If you are far behind and constantly struggling, try something else. Sometimes when the score is close, an unexpected hard serve or surprise serve will give you the edge. If you are serving well and scoring points, don't let up, because when your opponent gets to serve, he may have an equally successful run of points.

Ready Position for Receiving Serve (Figures 46 and 47)

To ready yourself for each serve, take a position near the center line of the service court and stand alertly with your weight evenly distributed on the balls of your feet. Your back foot should face the side wall and the front foot should be diagonal to the side wall. The feet are apart just enough to give good balance, but not so far that movement is restricted. Knees should be slightly flexed and easy, ready for instantaneous action. Your body is crouched rather than upright. The racquet is held at head height to the front and side of the body to allow a swift strike. Your eyes should be on your opponent to determine the type of serve he is planning to use. As soon as this is determined, fix your eyes on the ball to ascertain its direction. Then move! Go out and volley it if at all possible; otherwise, you will have to contend with the walls.

Return of Serve

The return of serve is undoubtedly as important as the serve since it is the receiver's first chance to play the ball. He is on the defensive, and it is imperative for him to play a shot that will establish him on an equal basis with the server, that is, transpose. The better the serve, the more difficult the receiver's task.

Which two shots would be best to play with the ball to X's right and the opponent at O? Which two shots would be best with the ball to X's left and the opponent at O?

Evaluation Questions
CHOOSING YOUR SHOT

To return a poor serve—one that has no speed and is away from the wall—go for a winner. A crosscorner shot is one of the most effective returns in this case because the ball goes to the corner farthest from the

Figure 46—Ready Position for Receiving Serve in Right Court.

Figure 47—Ready Position for Receiving Serve in Left Court.

Diagram B:

CHOOSING YOUR SHOT

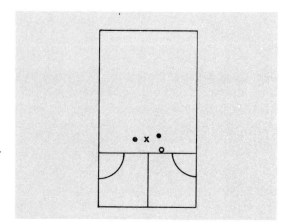

server's box. (See Figure 48.) A corner shot is a poor choice here because a corner is played into your own side wall and it would go to the server's side of the court. A better return would be to volley the ball straight down the wall just above the telltale. These shots with a low trajectory could be fortified with an attacking lob shot. It has speed, and its trajectory is between that of a drive and a defensive lob.

More important is how to return the difficult serve. A good lob serve is deep, and therefore you must transpose by playing your hardest drives or controlled lob very close down the wall with good length to deep corner. Keep alert and try not to panic when the odd serves come at you. You will acquire poise with experience. The tendency is to send odd serves back crosscourt, but make an effort to avoid this by playing them along the wall on your side of the court.

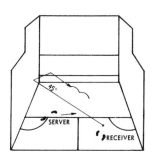

Figure 48—Forehand Crosscorner Return of Serve.

Position Play

Strategy is the process of outmaneuvering your opponent, thus enabling you to project the winning blow. The relationship of your position in the court to your opponent's is all important in your selection of shots. Note carefully in the Figures in Chapters 2 and 3 the positions of the two players (A, the stroker; B, the opponent) in the court. The ultimate aim of position play is to have the opponent behind and to one side of you. Repeatedly, the shot goes the farthest distance from B.

On a forehand corner (Figure 17), A is well aware that B is to his right and behind him, and he therefore must play the ball into the wall closest to himself. The wall shot (Figures 11 and 12) is played when opponent B is behind and cannot be seen in A's direct or peripheral vision. A shot played within your vision, therefore, must be logical, since your opponent isn't there. A crosscourt is played when your adversary anticipates your wall shot and is moving in that direction. It is useful, too, when an opponent crowds you closely and you wish to move him away into the other side of the court. To play a backhand crosscorner (Figure 31), your opponent should be visible to your right. The opponent is also visible to your right on a corner shot, but the crosscorner goes to the wall nearest him.

These position plays can be employed from front or backcourt. They are effective not only because they are the farthest distance from your opponent, but also because the stroker is on a line between the ball and the opponent. This is the reward for outmaneuvering your opponent! If there is any doubt as to choice, play a wall shot.

Often the speed of the exchanges makes it difficult to distinguish between an attacking and a defensive position. The two positions are not always clear-cut. Careful rotation around each other must take place in order to make the game enjoyable and safe.

In conclusion, determine your own capabilities and use them. Keep the ball in play and avoid outright errors into the telltale. Use a variety of strokes and tactics but attack your opponent's weakness. Above all, make the walls your friend!

DOUBLES

Although there are very few doubles courts in the world, a brief introduction to the game will be given here. Two players make up a team in doubles. Generally one plays on the right side of the court (forehand) and the other on the left side (backhand) but this does not prohibit the players from moving anywhere in the court should the necessity arise. Although the court is larger, the space is still congested with four players all trying to gain the center positions.

Note the serving and receiving positions in Figures 49 and 50. A1 is the server and the right court player; A2 is the server's partner and the left court player. B1 is the receiver and the left court player; B2 is the receiver's partner and the right court player.

Evaluation Questions

Can you bounce the ball on your racquet and cause it to spin clockwise, and then counterclockwise with a forehand? with a backhand?

A1 usually serves first to the backhand court player. Then A1, A2, and B2 move up towards the center of the court on their respective sides. When A1 serves from the left court, he must move quickly across to his side; however, no one should move to the center before the receiver has had a chance to make the return. The court positions of all the players depend on the direction of the receiver's return and subsequent returns. Refer to Chapter 7 for rules regarding serving order, etc.

The lob serve is the most common in doubles and after it is delivered, the four players jockey for positions at the T. The players having the right to the front position are the two opponents of the player stroking the ball. They should not be caught or be forced behind the stroker's partner. In other words, the stroker's partner cannot prevent either opponent from seeing or getting to the ball.

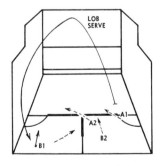

Figure 49—Doubles Serving from Right.

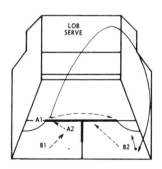

Figure 50—Doubles Serving from Left.

In doubles, exploit the weaker player. Work out a system with your partner to use your combined assets to best advantage. When both players have been forced forward or back and a space is wide open, hit for a winner quickly. In doubles, courtesy and racquet control are highly important in order to prevent injuries.

Whether playing singles or doubles, informally or competitively, your attitude towards the game will determine your enjoyment. In either situation, play to win, for that's the object. Confidence develops with sound knowledge and practice. If you do not practice, do not play in competition. Preparedness is the best pep talk. Be ready. As your confidence develops, excess tension disappears. A normal amount of tension is highly beneficial, as it indicates desire and keenness to succeed. When you take the court for a match, focus on the ball and pay attention to detail. If you forget about winning or losing at the moment and concentrate on the tactics of each point, the chances of a successful outcome of the match are increased. Those who enjoy playing are often successful.

In defeat, congratulate your opponent for the day, but get down to work tomorrow.

6

The Language and Lore of Squash Racquets

One of the several varieties of racquet (racket) sports was developed into "squash racquets" about the middle of the nineteenth century. The name, "squash," was probably given to the game because of the "mush" sound made when the soft ball, still used in England today, hit the wall; a sharp, cracking report, however, is made by a racquet's ball.

Although first mention of a game resembling squash was made in England in the thirteenth century, it was not until Dickens wrote "The Pickwick Papers" that mention was made of racquets being used in an indoor court, and then in a London debtors' prison, of all places! Indeed, the first out-of-prison racquets champion claimed to have learned the game in jail. This is greatly in contrast to modern squash racquet devotees, most of whom are members of private clubs.

It is believed that the first organized squash racquets game in the United States was played at St. Paul's School, Concord, New Hampshire, in 1882. The Philadelphia, Pennsylvania, Racquet Club claims the first known club squash court, built shortly after the opening of the PRC in 1890.

Equally as interesting as the history of the game is the definition of certain squash racquets terms.

Action—Rebound of the ball off the walls.

Appeal—Request made by player to the judges asking them to rule on a referee's questionable decision.

Attack—Offensive play usually in the forecourt.

Backcourt—Area behind the service line.

Backhand—Shots played on the left side of the body, for right-handed players.

Back Pedal—Moving backward with small quick steps.

Backswing—The motion taken in preparing to hit the ball.

Block—To interfere with an opponent's movements about the court.

Boast—A little-used desperation shot from a back corner traveling side wall, front wall, floor. Also called three-wall nick.

Bow—A little-used desperation shot from a back corner traveling side wall, side wall, front wall, floor.

Breaking—Undesirable rebound of the ball off the side wall after hitting the front wall.

Center Position—A position around the T where a player stands in relation to the lines of the court, the front wall, the opponent and the ball.

Chop—An undercut stroke.

Closed Stance—Feet parallel and pointing to the side wall.

Contact Point—The point at which the ball and racquet come in contact.

Corner Shot—Point winning shot traveling to side wall, front wall, floor.

Court—Area of play. See Figures 1 and 2.

Crease—The meeting point of the floor and a side or back wall.

Crosscorner—Point winning crosscourt shot traveling to side wall, front wall, floor.

Crosscourt Shots—Shots hit diagonally from one side of the court to the other.

CSRA—Canadian Squash Racquets Association.

Cut Line—Same as service line on front wall.

Deception—The art of deceiving or outwitting one's opponent, accomplished in squash racquets by changing the direction and speed of the wrist at the last minute.

Defense—Protection against an attack.

Double Hit—Hitting the ball twice in succession on the same stroke; an illegal procedure.

Doubles—Played by four people (two on a side) in a larger court and with a livelier ball than in singles.

Down—A shot hitting the telltale; same as not-up. Squash racquets etiquette requires a player to immediately call "down" or "not-up" when he has not hit the ball before the second bounce.

Drill—Repetitious exercises for developing skill.

Drive—A shot played with speed directly to the front wall after the ball has bounced.

Drop Shot—Finesse stroke hit with little speed and dropping close to the front wall. Sometimes called nick.

Eleonora Sears Perpetual Trophy—Trophy held by reigning USWSRA Singles Champions; formerly a three-win trophy retired by Margaret Varner in 1962, then returned to permanent competition by her in honor of the donor.

English Squash—Played on a larger court with a softer, smaller ball, a lighter racquet, and using a different scoring system. The court is 32 by 21 feet in size; front wall line 15 feet high; back wall line 7 feet high; front wall service line 6 feet high; telltale 19 inches high; floor service line 18 feet from front wall; service box 5 feet 3 inches square. The side wall limits are bounded by a straight line joining the front wall line to the back wall line. Scoring is similar to badminton in that points are scored only when serving. In singles 9 points, instead of 15, constitute a game. International matches are played according to the rules of the country in which the matches take place.

Face of Racquet—Area of contact with the ball; the strings.

Fault—A serve that hits on or below the service line, outside the court boundaries, or bounces outside the service court area.

Flat—The angle of the face of the racquet when not imparting spin.

Follow-through—The part of a stroke after the ball is hit which gives direction and control.

Foot Fault—Stepping on the line while serving, or lifting the foot off the floor before contacting the ball.

Forecourt—Area in the front of the court.

Forehand—Shots played on the right side of the body for right-handed players.

Gallery—Space behind the court where spectators and officials sit.

Game—A game unit consists of 15 points. See "setting."

Get—A scrambling return of a difficult shot.

Grant Trophy—In 1945, Canadian Alistair Grant presented this handsome trophy for competition; held in conjunction with the Lapham Cup.

Grip—Method of holding the racquet.

Half Volley—Ball contact immediately following its bounce.

Head of Racquet—The round part of the racquet containing the strings.

Hinder—To block or restrict an opponent from getting to or stroking the ball, resulting in a let or let point.

Howe Cup—Honors the most renowned family in USWSRA; Mrs. William F. Howe, Jr. and her twin daughters Elizabeth and Margaret, all three former national champions.

In Play—The ball is said to be "in play" from the time it is struck by the server's racquet until it hits out of bounds, or a fault or let occurs.

In Side—Serving side in doubles.

Judges—Two officials assisting the referee.

Kahn—Some member of this famous family, originally from Karachi, Pakistan, usually wins the world's major open championships. All are noted for their cat-like speed and superior mastery over the racquet and ball. Some first names are Hashim, Roshan, Azam and Mohibullah.

Ketcham Trophy—Men's Doubles Tri-City competition held in conjunction with the Lockett Cup. Presented by William T. Ketcham, Jr.

Kill—Fast shot which cannot be returned; a put-away.

Lapham Cup—Donated in 1922 by Boston's Henry G. Lapham to further international competition and good will in squash racquets.

Length—A ball which dies at the back wall.

Let—Legitimate cessation of play to allow an exchange or rally to be replayed. See illustrations and rules in Chapter 7.

Let Point—The awarding of a point rather than a replay of the point. See Chapter 7.

Lines—Balls striking a line are considered fault or out of court, the opposite of tennis.

Lob—A high arching deep underhand defensive stroke.

Lob Service—Underhand method of starting play.

Lockett Trophy—Intercity men's singles competition between New York, Philadelphia, and Boston.

Love—No score. English pronunciation of the French word "l'oeuf" meaning goose egg or zero.

Mask—To disguise the intention of a shot.

Match—Best three out of five games.

Midcourt—Area around the T or center position.

NAPSRA—North American Professional Squash Racquets Association.

Nick—Synonymous with drop shot or an unreturnable ball striking crease.

No Set—Electing not to extend the length of a game.

Not-up—Ball played after second bounce; same as down.

Open Stance—Position of the feet with the front foot pointing diagonally forward; back foot pointing to the side wall; front foot further from side wall than back foot.

Out of Court—Balls hitting the telltale or outside court boundaries.

Out Side—Receiving side in doubles.

Overarm Serves—Variety serves played above shoulder level.

Point—Smallest unit in scoring.

Point of Aim—A spot on the wall at which the ball is directed to obtain the desired angle and result.

Push Out—Process of moving around a back corner to have ample room to play the ball. The opponent must then move back and away from center.

Put-away—An unreturnable shot.

Racquets—The forerunner of squash racquets which is played on a larger court but with the same basic principles.

Rally—A series of shots.

Ready Position—Stance taken to receive serve.

Referee—The official who rules on questions of play such as lets, not-ups, etc.

Reverse Corner—A crosscorner shot.

Scorekeeper—Official who keeps the score and generally runs the game.

Sears, Eleonora R.—Colorful sports celebrity from Boston who was the first national women's singles champion; served 13 years as President of the USWSRA.

Serve or Service—Act of putting the ball into play. Opening stroke of each play or rally.

Service Box—Area from which the serve must be delivered.

Service Courts—Areas into which serve must be delivered—right and left courts.

Setting—Method of extending games by increasing the number of points necessary to win tied games. Player reaching tied score first has option of setting. Further described in Chapter 7.

Set-up—Poor shot which makes a put-away easy for the opponent. Also, placing the ball in a location necessary to practice a particular shot.

Side—A team of two players.

Side Out—Doubles term used to indicate that both players have completed their term of service and have become the receivers.

Sidespin—Stroking around the outside of the ball.

Slice—Combination of sidespin and underspin stroke.

Slice Service—A serve used in variation with the hard serve, preventing a volley.

Spin—Applying the racquet head to the ball at various angles.

Squash Racquets—A game in which a maximum amount of energy is expended in a minimum amount of time.

Stroke—Action of striking the ball with the racquet.

T—Center position around the service line.

Telltale—The low boundary area from the floor to a point 17 inches high on front wall made of sheet metal. Called the tin.

Time-out—Rest periods allowed between games.

Timing—Use of the wrist at contact point.

Tin—The telltale.

Touch—The player's finesse in stroking.

Transposition—Interchanging positions on the court during the course of a rally.

Turning on the Ball—An extreme emergency method of playing the ball off the back wall.

Underhand—Shots played below waist level.

Underspin—Chopping under the ball with an open faced racquet, causing the ball to rotate backwards.

USSRA—United States Squash Racquets Association, founded in 1920.

USWSRA—United States Women's Squash Racquets Association, organized in 1932.

Volley—Stroking the ball in the air before it touches the floor.

Wall Shot—Also called down-the-line, rail, or alley shot. A ball which travels close to and parallel to the side wall.

Warm-up—Practice period before the match begins.

Wightman, Hazel Hotchkiss—World famous tennis champion who won the National Squash Racquets Championship in 1930 from Eleonora Sears. During a hard fought rally Miss Sears was quoted as saying "Get out of my way," to which Mrs. Wightman replied "I can't. You're on my foot!"

Winner—Same as put-away or kill.

Wolfe-Noel Cup—The privilege of donating this international cup was won by the flip of a coin in 1933 by Englishwomen Elizabeth Wolfe and Susan Noel over Eleonora Sears.

7

Rules of the Game

Although an official rule book should be consulted for tournament play, the following set of rules with explanations and examples for clarification will suffice for scholastic and recreational play. The United States Squash Racquets Association has established rules pertinent to the court, equipment, players, service, method of scoring, etc.

SINGLES

1. *Server*—At the start of a match, opposing players spin a racquet to determine who is to serve and who is to receive first. The winner of the spin has the choice. The player winning the first game chooses whether he wants to serve or receive first in the second game. In singles, almost without exception, a player elects to serve first.

2. *Service*—A ball is in play from the moment it is served until a point is decided, a fault is made, or a let occurs.

   At the beginning of a game, and each time there is a new server, the server may elect to serve from either service box. The next serve, however, must be from the other service box and thereafter alternately until the serve is lost or the game is completed. For example, if a player starts serving from the right service box and scores a point, he must next serve from the left service box. If the server serves from the wrong box and the receiver does not attempt to return the serve, he can demand that the serve be from the correct box. The referee calls a let, and the play is started from the correct box.

The server must follow certain rules when serving. One foot must be on the floor inside the service box and not touch any lines when the serve is delivered. If the server violates this rule, he is committing a foot fault. After the moment of impact of the ball and racquet, his foot may be moved anywhere. It is not illegal to have both feet in the box, but it is not good technique. The server must serve the ball so that it first strikes the front wall above the service line and below the 16 foot line. It must then rebound and strike the floor in the correct service court either before or after touching the side or back walls if the receiver elects to allow it to hit. A ball not served in this manner is considered a fault.

If the first service is a fault or if a foot fault is committed, the server serves again from the same side. If the second serve is also a fault or foot fault, the server loses the point and his opponent serves.

A service called a fault may not be played. However, a player may elect to volley (strike the ball before it bounces) a serve. There is then the possibility that a player who volleys could play a serve that would eventually have been a fault. Correct judgment in this case is essential.

3. *Return of Service and Subsequent Play*

   a. To make a legal return of serve, the ball may be either volleyed or struck before it has bounced twice on the floor. It must then be returned to the front wall above the telltale. Any ball hitting the front wall below a height of 17 inches is out of play. The ball may strike any wall or walls before or after it hits the front wall. A return is considered to be made at the moment of contact of the ball with the racquet of the player making the return.

   b. If the receiver fails to make a good return the server wins the point. If the receiver does make a good return, the players alternate making returns until one fails to do so. The player who does not make a good return loses the point.

   c. The players may make any number of good returns as long as the ball does not bounce twice or touch either of them.

   d. If the ball hits outside the court boundaries, on the boundary line or hits the ceiling, lights or the telltale, a fault is called. The player hitting such a ball loses the point. The exception is on service when, if the first serve is a fault, a second one may be attempted.

How should O and X rotate if a good wall shot, crosscourt, drop shot or crosscorner is played by O from the forecourt? from the midcourt? from the backcourt?

Evaluation Questions

ROTATING YOUR POSITION

4. *Score*—Each point won by a player adds one to his score.

5. *Game*—The player who first scores 15 points wins the game except when "setting" occurs. "Setting" is a method of extending the length of a game if it is tied at a particular score. See the chart below.

Points in game	Score set at	Points required to win game
15	13 all for 5	18
	13 all for 3	16
	No set	15
15	14 all for 3	17
	No set	15

The player reaching the tied score first decides whether to set the score. If he elects not to set the score, the conventional number of points (15) completes the game. A player not setting the score at the first opportunity may set the score should the occasion arise again. For example: If the score is tied at 13 all and the player who reached 13 first calls "no set," play supposedly continues to 15. If the play is tied at 14 all, whichever player reached 14 first is offered the opportunity to set the score. Assuming that that player is the one who called "no set" at 13 all, he may this time elect to set the score to 3.

6. *Match*—A match is the best three out of five games.

7. *Keep Out of Opponent's Way* (Figures 51, 52, 53, and 54)—Each player must move out of his opponent's way as soon as he has struck the ball. By moving out of the way, he gives his opponent

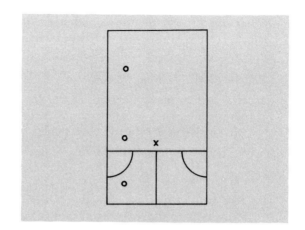

Diagram C:

ROTATING YOUR
POSITION

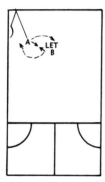

*Figure 51—Let
Situation—Front Court.*

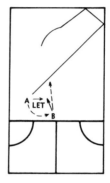

*Figure 52—Let
Situation—Midcourt.*

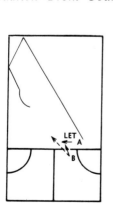

*Figure 53—Let
Situation—Midcourt.*

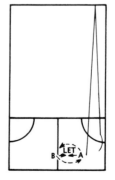

*Figure 54—Let
Situation—Backcourt.*

a fair opportunity to run to and strike the ball from any part of the court. He must also take a position that allows his opponent to hit any part of the front wall or hit either side wall near the front wall.

8. *Ball in Play Touching Player*

   a. If a ball in play *after* hitting the front wall touches either player or anything they wear or carry (except the racquet of the player who makes the return), that player loses the point. If the striker is in a location that prohibits his opponent from getting out of the way of the ball, however, a let occurs. This situation seldom occurs.

   b. If a ball in play touches the player who last returned it or anything he wears or carries *before* it hits the front wall, that player loses the point. This situation rarely occurs.

   c. If a ball in play *after* it is struck and on its way to the front wall hits the striker's opponent or anything he wears or carries, various rulings may apply. The player who made the return that touched his opponent loses the point if the return would not have been good regardless. If, however, the ball would have gone *directly* to the front wall without touching any other walls, a point is awarded. Obviously a player cannot stand in front of his opponent's shots and claim a let. A shot may be a winner, and the opponent would therefore be "robbed" of a point. However, the point is replayed as a let if the ball would have hit the side wall and then the front wall if it had not touched the opponent first. It would also be a let if the ball hit a side wall and then touched the opponent before going to the front wall. In conclusion, when interference of this sort occurs, a point is awarded for balls going directly to the front wall, but a let is played if the ball was going to or from the side wall. When there is no referee, and the players cannot agree whether or not the ball was going to the front wall, then the point is replayed. Under no circumstances does play continue after the ball touches a player or his effects.

9. *Let*—A let is the stopping of play and the playing over of a point. On the replay the server:

   a. is entitled to the two serves even though his first serve was a fault on the original point;

   b. must serve from the correct box even though it was discovered he served from the wrong box on the original point; and

   c. may, if he is a new server, serve from either service box.

Other lets occur during play. A let is called when:

a. a player unavoidably gets in his opponent's way and restricts him from moving to any part of the court or restricts him from fairly or easily playing the ball;

b. a player does not stroke the ball for fear of contacting and perhaps injuring his opponent;

c. the player's racquet, his clothing, or the player himself is touched by the opponent when he is preparing or in the act of striking the ball. In other words, players may inadvertently touch each other in the process of running about the court without interfering with each other, which is perfectly legal. If this happens during the stroking process, however, a let situation occurs. Interference in the stroking alters the effect on the ball, and in most cases a poor shot is produced.

d. a ball, after the first bounce, bounces exceptionally high and hits out of bounds on the back wall. An occurrence such as this would not give a player a fair play on the ball.

e. a ball breaks in play; if during play, a player suspects the ball has broken, he should finish the point and then check the ball. If the ball has broken, the point is replayed.

If the referee fails to call a let when in the opinion of a player he is entitled to a let, the player can appeal to the referee. The referee determines if a let did or did not occur and gives his decision. This decision is final. There is never a let on a nick regardless of a player's obstruction or block.

The referee can call a let for any interference in the play not caused by either player. For instance, if a spectator drops something into the playing area, the referee calls a let.

10. *Let Point*—A let point occurs when a point is awarded because of unnecessary interference with an opponent in his playing of a point or unnecessary crowding as defined in Rule 7. Even though the opposing player was not actually prevented from reaching or playing the ball, the referee must award the point to the player unnecessarily interfered with. The purpose of this rule is to prevent rough and unsporting play. For example, a player having a chance to score a point or "put away" the ball is unnecessarily interfered with by his opponent. To call a let in this instance equalizes the situation when in actuality it penalizes the player on the verge of scoring.

If a player feels he is entitled to a let point which has not been called, he should at once appeal to the referee for a decision. This situation demands fine sportsmanship. Unnecessary crowding is a difficult subjective judgment made by the referee, and the players should avoid placing the referee in such a position. Quite often an entire match is played with no lets or let points. Most lets should only happen unintentionally when the ball takes an unintended rebound.

11. *Continuity of Play*—Play must be continuous from the first service of each game until the game is concluded. There may be an interval of one minute between games if requested by one or both of the players. An interval of five minutes between the third and fourth games is permissible if requested. If neither player asks for these rest periods, play continues. Players cannot leave the court except during the five minute interval unless given permission by the referee.

The referee suspends play in the event either player is injured. If the injured player cannot resume playing within an hour, he must default the match.

Play cannot be stopped to permit a player to rest, to get his wind, or to regain strength. The referee is the sole judge of intentional delay for any reason and he must give due warning if this infraction occurs. If it continues, the offender is disqualified.

Players and officials should pay serious attention to the rules related to continuity of play in order to make playing conditions fair to both players.

If play has to be suspended for some reason beyond the control of all, such as the failure of the lighting system, play continues when the correction is made. If it is impossible to continue play within an hour, the match is rescheduled. It is then resumed from the point and game score existing when it was unavoidably stopped unless the referee and both players unanimously agree to play the entire match or any part of it over.

12. *Attire and Equipment*—A player's complete attire must be white. Any controversy over attire is under the jurisdiction of the referee.

The USSRA states the specifications of an official singles ball. It shall be made of black rubber and be 1.700 to 1.750 inches in diameter. It shall weigh 1.12 to 1.17 ounces and be pneumatic (inflated with air). The rebound of the ball is very important. At a temperature of 70 to 74 degrees Fahrenheit, it must rebound off a steel plate from

24 to 26 inches when dropped from a height of 100 inches. At a temperature of 83 to 84 degrees Fahrenheit, it must rebound from 27 to 30 inches. It is estimated that after ten minutes of play the ball's temperature increases just over ten degrees. The difference in the amount of rebound can affect the speed and type of game to be played. A ball is considered unsatisfactory if it has more than a 20 per cent increase in rebound before and after ten minutes of play. Obviously the temperature of the court and the ball is important.

The racquet is constructed of wood with a circular head with a maximum diameter of nine inches. The over-all length should not exceed 27 inches and the racquet weighs approximately nine to ten ounces. It may be strung with gut or synthetic material but not with metal. See Figure 3 in Chapter 1.

13. *Condition of the Ball*—The temperature of the ball cannot be artificially changed before or during a match. It cannot be heated or chilled to suit a particular player's desires in hopes of raising the standard of his game.

Any time the ball is not in actual play, another ball may be substituted if the players mutually consent to a change or the referee considers it necessary.

At the present time, ball manufacturing companies are experimenting with different speeds of balls. Because the type of game varies so greatly from a hot to a cold court, the problem is to find a ball to equalize the situation, that is, to provide a fast ball for a cold court and a slow ball for a hot court. Opponents of such a plan contend that variation in temperature and its implications are what make the game interesting and thought-provoking.

14. *Condition of the Court*—See Figures 1 and 2 in Chapter 1 for details and dimensions of the squash court. The court must be empty except for the players, their clothing, their racquets, and the ball. All other equipment such as extra balls, extra racquets, sweaters not being worn, towels, etc. must be left outside the court. A player who requires a towel or cloth to wipe his eyeglasses should keep it in his pocket or attach it to his belt or waist.

15. *Referee*—A referee controls the game as soon as the players enter the court. Players can warm up any length of time provided they are ready to play when the match is scheduled to start. However, the referee may limit the warm-up period just prior to the match to five minutes.

Occasionally two judges are appointed in addition to the referee. These judges make their decisions when a player appeals (or questions) the referee's decision. The point in question is therefore acted upon by three persons and the majority opinion prevails. The judges are not called upon to make any decisions unless an appeal has been made by a player. The referee announces the decision promptly.

Most of the rules that apply to singles also apply to doubles. Some rules, however, differ because of the increased size of the court. Unless otherwise stated, the playing rules are the same.

FROM THE METROPOLITAN (N.Y.) S.R.A.
1967 - 68 YEARBOOK

The following is a brief discussion of the purposes and concepts of the new Rules recently (Oct. 1967) promulgated by the United States Squash Racquets Association. The italics in the discursive paragraphs are the Editor's, to highlight important facets. The actual changes are appended.

Rule 7 has been amended to clarify the obligations of a player after he has made his shot. A player must keep entirely clear of his opponent's shot *from whatever position his opponent may wish to play the shot and whenever he may wish to play it.* An opponoent is not obliged to adjust his positional play to a particular player's style of play.

Rule 9 has been amended to achieve three specific aims: (1) to prevent a referee from being too hasty in calling a Let when there is contact between the players, thereby stopping play and depriving a player of continuing through with a shot which he feels has a good chance of being a winning one; (2) to assure a player's right to a Let if he has been disturbed by his opponent, even though there may have been no contact or touching between the players or their racquets; and (3) to eliminate the burden on players who don't like to ask for Let Points, by providing that *a request for a Let automatically includes a request for a Let Point.*

Rule 10 clarifies the Let Point. *A player must make the necessary effort* within the scope of his normal ability to avoid causing a Let. Fatigue is no excuse. If a player fails to make such effort and thereby deprives his opponent of a clear opportunity to attempt a winning shot, it is a Let Point against him. Even if he hasn't deprived his opponent of a chance for a winner, *it is a Let Point against him if he has repeatedly caused Lets* previously during the match under similar circumstances. This should discourage the constant "crowder" and those who consistently fail to "clear" after making their own shots.

Rule 15 (c) is designed *to put an end to all the argument from the players* during a match. The referee can always inquire if he is at all uncertain why a given request for a Let or Let Point or an Appeal has been made.

In summary, the changes are intended to bring the language of rules in line with the high standards of sportsmanship and conduct of play which makes the game of squash racquets a challenge for the players and a pleasure for the spectators.

The following material shows only the Rules or sub-divisions thereof which are actually changed. The parts which are new appear in italics.

7. Keep Out of Opponent's Way
    (b) Must give his opponent a fair opportunity to get to and/or strike at the ball *in any position on the court elected by his opponent;*
    (c) Must allow his opponent to play the ball from any parts of the court *elected by his opponent;* and . . .

9. Let
    (a) *When a player violates Rule 7;* (Note: the word "unavoidably" has been deleted.)

The following part of Rule 9 is all new, commencing with the paragraph following (f), and replacing all the remainder of the Rule:

The referee may not call or allow a Let under this Rule 9 unless such Let is requested by a player; provided, however, that the referee may call a Let at any time (1) when there is interference with play caused by any factor beyond the control of the players or (2) when he fears that a player is about to suffer severe physical injury.

No Let shall be allowed on any stroke a player makes unless he requests such Let before or in the act of striking at the ball.

A player may request a Let or a Let Point. A request by a player for a Let shall automatically include a request for a Let Point. Upon such request, the referee shall allow a Let, Let Point, or No Let.

10. Let Point
    A Let Point is the unnecessary violation of Rule 7 (b), 7 (c) or 7 (d). An unnecessary violation occurs (1) when the player fails to

make the necessary effort within the scope of his normal ability to avoid the violation, thereby depriving his opponent of a clear opportunity to attempt a winning shot, or (2) when the player has repeatedly failed to make the necessary effort within the scope of his normal ability to avoid similar violations. The player unnecessarily violating Rule 7 (b), 7 (c) or 7 (d) loses the point.

15. Referee

    Note: The following new material constitutes an added paragraph.

    (c) *A player shall not state his reasons for his request under Rule 9 for a Let or Let Point or for his appeal from any decision of the referee or judges, provided, however, that the referee may request the player to state his reasons.*

DOUBLES

1. *Sides*—Each side or team consists of two players.

2. *Server*—The serving side is referred to as the "in" side and the receiving side as the "out" side. Both players on a team serve in succession. The first server serves and continues serving until his side loses a point; then his partner serves. As long as points are being scored, this second server continues serving. When he loses a point, both players on the other team take turns at serving.

    At the beginning of each game, only one player on a team gets to serve before it is "side-out," and then both players on the opposing team serve. This is a peculiarity of the serving order of the doubles game which is found in badminton also. In both games it is considered an advantage to serve, but often the team which won the spin of the racquet and has the choice of serving and receiving will elect to receive first.

    The order of serving within a side is not changed during the progress of a game. In other words, if A served followed by B, then each time their sides serve, A must serve first. This order can be changed at the end of the game.

    At the end of a game the side which won the first game has the choice of serving or receiving to begin the next game.

3. *Service*—At the beginning of each game and each time a side begins its turn at serving, it has the choice of serving from either service box. The next serve must be from the other service box and thereafter continue alternately as points are scored. In other words, it

is possible to choose which player you wish to serve first but no player may be served to twice in succession. Usually the serve is directed to the weaker player first.

4. *Return of Service and Subsequent Play*—At the beginning of each game, a team decides which player is to receive service in the right-hand service court and which player will receive in the left-hand service court and they must continue receiving service in their designated courts that entire game. At the end of the game, this receiving order may be changed.

5. *Attire and Equipment*—The standard doubles ball of the USSRA is made of rubber 1¾ inches in diameter and weighs from 1 to 1.06 ounces. It must be pneumatic and have a rebound upon a steel plate at a temperature of 68 degrees Fahrenheit of 36 inches from a drop of 100 inches.

The doubles ball rebounds to a much greater degree than the singles ball, a necessity because the doubles court is considerably larger. It is, in fact, 6 feet 6 inches wider and 13 feet longer. It is interesting to note that the difference in the two balls also gives a different "feeling" to the ball as it contacts the racquet.

8

Unwritten Rules

Like all sports, squash racquets has unwritten as well as written rules. Traditionally, squash racquets has been played by ladies and gentlemen whose conduct has been much admired.

White clothing is the traditional color for the racquet sports and for good reason in squash racquets. Since the ball is small and black and usually travels at a fast pace, it can be very difficult to see. If a player wears dark clothing, the ball becomes lost to the eye as the opponent plays the ball. It is very important to see the ball and determine its direction at the earliest possible moment.

Customary courtesies are associated with informal or match play. A few cordial words passed back and forth between players before the game begins makes for a pleasant occasion. Players should always bring one or two balls with them and perhaps a towel. Any extra equipment should be left outside the court.

During the warm-up preceding a game, the sportsmanship and courteousness of one's opponent can easily be determined. The purpose of the warm-up is for the players to hit the ball back and forth to each other in order to warm up the ball as well as themselves. The serve should be practiced also. A player who hits unretrievable shots, practices particular shots, and hits up and down his side wall keeps his opponent from warming up. If a player wishes to practice these particular shots before a match, he should practice them in another court. In the warm-up with your opponent, the crosscourt shot is the only shot that can be hit to your opponent. The hope is that it will be returned in the same manner. The end result is that both players then stroke enough balls to get the feel of the ball and determine its action in the particular court.

Once the game starts, fairness on the part of both players should prevail. If either hits the ball out of bounds, he should quickly call "out." If his shot should hit the telltale and be inaudible, he should call "down" instantly. A "not-up" call should be forthcoming if he plays the ball after the second bounce. A prompt call in the aforementioned circumstances made before the opponent has played the ball is highly desirable.

The swing of the racquet in squash must be a smaller swing than that made by the tennis racket. This is because the court is small and both players must maneuver around each other in a very confined area. Limiting one's backswing and follow-through gives a bit more space in which to maneuver. It also lessens the chance of injury and undoubtedly makes for more correct and accurate stroking. Players with big, wild swings often find it difficult to locate opponents who will play with them. Keep the follow-through below shoulder level. If the opponent is hit it bruises. Hit above the shoulder level the follow-through annihilates!

A squash racquets rule states that if a ball going directly to the front wall strikes your opponent, the striker wins the point. Here is an opportunity not only to show good sportsmanship but also to prevent injury. Call a let before stroking the ball. Only a few persons intentionally place themselves in front of a ball to save a point. If this occurs during a match, a good referee can control such antics; if it is in practice, it makes no difference. It is only a game and one's reputation is of more value. Some players are known for hitting the ball regardless of the situation. This sort of behavior detracts from the fun of the game, and is extremely poor sportsmanship.

During the game, many opportunities occur to demonstrate good manners and sportsmanship. These arise because both players are on the same side of the "net" and must rotate around each other. This maneuvering requires a great deal of cooperation and consideration of the other person. A player should stroke the ball and quickly move out of the way, allowing his opponent to have a free chance to hit the ball. If he is near the ball when his opponent is attempting to play it, he must allow him to stroke it with ease and without interference. The unsporting player hits the ball and stands planted to block his opponent from getting to the ball. Squash is not football! It is obvious to one's opponent whether he has been blocked or subtly interfered with. Chapter 7 clarifies how a player should move to give his adversary a fair chance to reach and to play the ball.

A very clever and unsporting maneuver that many players indulge in is that of hitting a shot at such an angle that it arrives back directly in front of themselves. Such a shot is perfectly acceptable provided the player moves out of the way in order to give his opponent a fair chance to play the ball. Over and over again this situation occurs, and the player making the shot misleads himself into thinking his superior shot rather than his blocking tactics won the point. The opponent could technically ask for a let, but calling innumerable lets detracts from the enjoyment of the game.

Keeping score continually and correctly if you are without a referee makes a smoother game with less chance of disagreement. Banging the racquet about and emotional outbursts have no place on the squash court. Don't encourage your opponent by showing anger! The opponent's or referee's decision on a play is generally accepted without question. Always shake hands with your opponent at the conclusion of a match and thank the referee who has officiated.

Off the court certain niceties are associated with the game. Be on time! If you enter a tournament, submit your entry on time, pay your entry fee promptly, and arrive on time for your match. Thank your opponent for the match; remember the score and give it to the official at the conclusion of your match. Then find out when your next match is scheduled. If you have been a guest at a club or in a home, be sure to thank those who have shown you courtesy.

In individual, school, and club play, those players who violate the unwritten rules of etiquette seldom find opponents, and those who do agree to play with such players do so with considerable caution!

9

Facts for
Enthusiasts

The squash court is an interesting and expensive playing area with walls constructed of wood that gives a true rebound and will withstand the punishment of a hard squash ball. A top quality court costs thousands of dollars, and expense is therefore one of the limiting aspects of the game. Successful experiments have been made using cement and synthetic materials for wall surfaces to lessen the expense; as a result, today more and more schools and clubs are installing courts. Another factor which in the past has limited the widespread growth of the game is the amount of spectator space allowable. This space, the gallery, is usually found behind the court since the back wall is at a considerably lower height than the other three walls. Limited spectator space diminishes the possibility of revenue which could in turn be invested in the game for its growth. It can be concluded that those who do play squash play for the enjoyment of the game rather than for money derived from it!

The court with its four walls makes for an interesting game because various angles and shots develop in the course of a point. In addition, the variation in temperature of courts causes changes in the game. The recommended court temperature is 40 degrees because of the sustained speed and explosiveness of the game. Many courts are located in YMCA's, clubs, and downtown office buildings where temperatures are usually kept between 65 and 70 degrees. Imagine the expense of installing cooling systems to lower the squash court temperature in these buildings! Some clubs have squash courts in separate unheated buildings because it is more economical not to use heat. The temperature of these courts is subject to natural weather conditions. With this constant change in court temperature, and the concurrent change in the temperature of the ball (hot court: fast ball, cold court: dead ball) the game changes. This is what makes squash an interesting game and demands thought, awareness, and resourcefulness on the part of a player who must adapt to such differing conditions.

The ball is a very hard rubber object about the size of a golf ball that can be devastating in its effects—especially when it comes in contact with a player! At the present time, a squash ball sells for about one dollar. It usually lasts a good length of time, and many players play an entire season with only three or four balls. Balls are the least expensive aspect of the game. Various companies are developing varying speeds of balls to suit different temperatures, since there are occasions when a squash court can become so hot or so cold that enjoyment of the game is impossible.

The racquet is made of wood and has a comparatively long handle. It weighs between nine and ten ounces and is somewhat heavier though smaller in the head than a tennis or badminton racquet. The balance of a racquet can vary from "head heavy" to "light in the head." A head heavy racquet will add power to the strokes, but it cannot be moved to position as quickly as a racquet that is light in the head. The handle is narrow and the grip is covered with leather. It is strung very tightly with gut or nylon, and sells from about $7.00 to $30.00.

In selecting a racquet, decide how much you are prepared to pay, examine the various models in that range, and try a few practice swings. When you find a racquet that "feels" comfortable, that's the one to select. A beginner should solicit the aid of a teacher to determine the correct weight and balance.

A good racquet under normal use and care should last about two seasons. When not in use it should be kept in a press and stored in a cool, dry place.

Since there is a great deal of running forward and back, and twisting and turning quickly in squash, a good pair of tennis shoes and one or two pairs of clean socks are of the utmost importance. A sturdy pair of shoes is more expensive, but well worth the investment.

White clothing—shoes, socks, shorts, shirt, and sweater—should be loose fitting to allow freedom of movement, and above all the clothing should be kept clean.

10

Playing the Game

Although squash racquets is a minor sport in the United States and one which in the past has been played only by those able to afford membership in a club having squash courts, it is becoming increasingly popular. More people are becoming acquainted with the game and realizing its values. A 45-minute workout in squash is ample daily exercise for anyone.

The three governing organizations of squash racquets in the United States are the United States Squash Racquets Association, the United States Women's Squash Racquets Association, and the North American Professional Squash Racquets Association. The Canadian Squash Racquets Association administers the game in Canada. An individual who plays or is interested in squash is encouraged to take a membership in one of these organizations. Membership allows players to enter sanctioned tournaments and receive bulletins and yearbooks published by the association. The USSRA publishes an excellent official yearbook which can be obtained from the secretary. It lists the individual and club members, tournament schedule, tournament results, national rankings, historical information, various regional reports, and the official rules.

The first national men's championship was played in 1907; the first women's championship in 1928. Since then various other championship singles and doubles events have been added: intercollegiate, senior (over 40 years of age), junior (under 18 years of age), team, open, professional. There are annual Lapham Cup singles matches and Grant Cup doubles matches with Canada, with England invited to send a team.

In the women's activities, the Howe Cup intercity matches are of annual interest. The Wolfe-Noel matches are five singles matches played every three years between the women of England and the United States.

It is interesting to note that in the open championships for men both amateurs and professionals are allowed to compete, an unheard of occurrence in tennis and badminton.

PREPARING A SQUASH DRAW

Seeding—There shall be no more than one seeded player for every four players in the draw. A draw of 16, therefore, may have no more than four seeded players; a draw of 32 may have no more than eight seeded players, etc. All seeded players are placed at the top of their respective halves, quarters, or eighths of the draw. Number one seed shall be in the top half and number two seed in the lower half. Number three and four seed shall be drawn by lot to determine which is placed in the upper and lower halves. Likewise, numbers five, six, seven and eight shall be drawn by lot to determine their respective locations by quarters. If there is a foreign seed, the foreign seeded players are arranged in reverse order on the above system, i.e. the number one foreign seed is placed at the bottom of the draw.

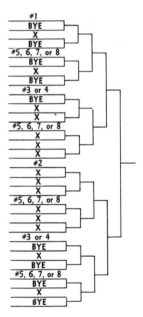

Byes—If the number of entries is a power of 2 (4, 8, 16, 32, etc.) no byes are necessary. If the number of entries is not a power of two, the number of byes required is obtained by subtracting the number of entries from the next higher power of two. In the example draw there are 23 entries. The next higher power of two is 32, thereby giving nine byes. If the number of byes is even, half are placed at the top of the draw and half at the bottom. If the number of byes is odd, one more bye is placed at the top of the draw than at the bottom. Byes are concentrated at the top and bottom of the draw and not distributed throughout. See example draw (Figure 55).

Figure 55—Example Draw.

Selected References

BOOKS

Barnaby, John M. *Squash Rackets in Brief.* Lincoln, Mass.: J. M. Barnaby, 1961.

Butcher, D. G. *Introducing Squash.* London: Faber and Faber, Ltd., 1949.

Cowles, Harry. *The Art of Squash Racquets.* New York: The Macmillan Co., 1935.

Debany, Walter. *Squash Racquets.* New York: A. S. Barnes, 1950.

Giles, J. H. *Squash Rackets.* London: Nicholas Kaye Ltd., 1961.

Hankinson, J. T. *Squash Racquets.* New York: The Macmillan Co., 1946.

Hawkey, R. B. *New Angles on Squash.* London: Ward, Lock & Co., Ltd. 1951.

Molloy, Albert. *Sports Illustrated Book of Squash.* Philadelphia: J. B. Lippincott Co., 1963.

Moss, Major T., Edward Snell, and Capt. J. E. Tomkinson. *Squash Rackets.* London: Seeley Service & Co., Ltd., 1949.

Pawle, Gerald. *Squash Rackets.* London: Ward, Lock & Co., Ltd., 1951.

Phillips, Brian. *Tackle Squash Rackets This Way.* London: Stanley Paul & Co. Ltd., 1960.

Potter, Arthur M. *Squash Racquets.* Baltimore: John D. Lucas Printing Co., 1938.

Skillman, John. *Squash Racquets.* New York: McGraw-Hill Book Co., Inc., 1937.

Squash Rackets Association. *Know The Game Squash Rackets.* London: Educational Productions Ltd., 1950.

SELECTED REFERENCES

MAGAZINES AND PAMPHLETS

British Lawn Tennis Inc. Squash. C. M. Jones, Cheshire Court, 142 Fleet St., London, E.C.4, England.

Handbook. Squash Rackets Association, J. H. Horry, 137 Regent St., London, W.1, England.

Interclub Schedule. Philadelphia Women's Squash Racquets Association, Mrs. H. L. Clement, 21 Railroad Ave., Haverford, Pa. 19041

Official Handbook. United States Women's Squash Racquets Association, Miss Betty Shellenberger, 107 School House Lane, Philadelphia, Pa. 19144

Official Year Book. United States Squash Racquets Association, Inc., Darwin P. Kingsley III, 470 Latch's Lane, Merion, Pa. 19066

Squash Court Construction. D. B. Frampton & Co., Huntington Bank Bldg., Columbus, Ohio. 43215

Playing Rules. United States Squash Racquets Association, Inc., Darwin P. Kingsley III, 470 Latch's Lane, Merion, Pa. 19066

Squash Racquets, Who Plays?—and Where? Darwin P. Kingsley III, 470 Latch's Lane, Merion, Pa. 19066

Tournament Schedule. United States Women's Squash Racquets Association, Mrs. Hallett Johnson, Jr., Pretty Brook Road, Princeton, N.J. 08540

Tennis, Magazine of the Racquet Sports. P.O. Box 5, Ravinia Station, Highland Park, Illinois. 60035

Yearbook. Metropolitan Squash Racquets Association. Robert H. Lehman, 20 E. 46th St., New York, N.Y. 10017

SLIDES

USSRA Instructional Slides. Darwin P. Kingsley III, 470 Latch's Lane, Merion, Pa. 19066

ASSOCIATIONS

CSRA. Ian Stewart, 1 March St., Toronto, Canada.

NAPSRA. James Bentley, Toronto Cricket, Skating & Curling Club, 141 Wilson Ave., Toronto, Canada.

USSRA. William T. Ketcham, Jr., 821 United Nations Plaza, New York, N.Y. 10017

USWSRA. Miss Caroline Haussermann, 21 Sunset St., Chestnut Hill, Philadelphia, Pa. 19118

Index

action, 41
appeal, 41, 53, 56
associations, 68
attack, 34, 42
attire, 54, 60, 64

backhand, 42
backhand corner shot, 14
backhand crosscorner, 25
backhand drives, 9-12
backhand volley, 16
back pedal, 42
backwall drill, 30
balls, 2, 54-55, 64
ball breaks, 53
ball touches player, 52
block, 42
boast, 26, 42
books, 67
bow, 26, 42
breaking, 42
byes, 66

center position, 42
chop, 42
closed stance, 42
conditioning, 17-18
contact point, 42
continuity of play, 54
corner shots, 14-15, 42
corner shots to avoid, 15
court, 1-2, 42, 55, 63
crease, 42
crosscorner, 25, 42
crosscorner return of serve, 37
crosscourt drive drill, 32
crosscourt shot drills, 28-29, 31-32
crosscourt shots, 12-13, 42
crosscourt shots to avoid, 13
CSRA, 42, 65
cut line, 42

deception, 42
defense, 34, 43
double hit, 43
doubles, 38-40, 43
doubles balls, 59
doubles court, 2
doubles rules, 58-59
doubles serves, 58-59
down, 43, 61

draw, 66
drills, 28-33
drive, 43
drives, 9-12
dropshot, 23-24, 43

equipment, 2, 54
etiquette, 60-62

fault, 43
flat, 43
follow-through, 43
footwork, 17-18
forehand, 44
forehand corner shot, 15
forehand drive, 9-12
forehand dropshot, 24
forehand volley, 16
four stroke drill, 33

gallery, 44, 63
game, 2, 44, 50
get, 44
glossary, 41-47
Grant Trophy, 44, 65
grip, 5-6, 44

half volley, 44
hinder, 44, 50, 52-54
Howe Cup, 44, 66

in play, 3, 44
"in" side, 44, 58

judges, 44, 56

Kahn, 44
Ketcham Trophy, 44

Lapham Cup, 44, 65
length, 45
let, 45, 50-53
let point, 45, 53-54
lob, 25-26, 45
lob serve, 6-9, 45
lob serve flight patterns, 8
Lockett Trophy, 45
love, 45

magazines, 68
mask, 45

69